XTREME SPORTS

Cutting Edge

by E.J. Maxwell

XTREME SPORTS

Cutting Edge

by E.J. Maxwell

SCHOLASTIC INC.

New York   Toronto   London   Auckland   Sydney
Mexico City   New Delhi   Hong Kong   Buenos Aires

PHOTO CREDITS:
Cover, 67, 68, 76, 80: Icon Sports Photos. **7, 23, 37, 41, 57, 60:** Tony Donaldson/Icon SMI. **28:** STL/Icon SMI. **44, 48:** Paul Buckley/Icon SMI. **86:** Dennis Currin/Icon SMI. **91:** Bob Falcetti/Icon SMI. **13, 19:** Icon/Allsport.

ISBN 0-439-46854-X

12 11 10 9 8   6 7 8/0

Printed in the U.S.A.   40
First printing, January 2003
Book Design: Michael Malone

TABLE of CONTENTS

INTRODUCTION

Back in the old days, it was the golden-armed quarterback who was idolized. Or the sweet-shooting guard on the basketball team. Or the pitcher with a curveball that danced and a fast-ball that smoked. These were the professional athletes who stood as role models and heroes for kids and adults alike.

The guy defying gravity on his little bike? The girl doing backflips on her snowboard? They were in the shadows. No one really noticed their creativity and discipline. No one really cared. The media exposure and endorsement contracts went to the superstars in the superstar sports. Everything else was merely an alternative, and not a very attractive one at that.

My, how times have changed. In 2002, the snowboarder draws legions of fans to her every performance, and the bicycle stunt rider is so popular he has his own action figure. Kids across the country are as likely to spend their

Dave Mirra

afternoons at the local skate park as they are at the soccer field. It's a rad new world, one in which alternative sports aren't so alternative, and mainstream sports are being left in the dust. So get used to it.

"Extreme sports are catching up all over the world," observes freestyle BMX legend Dave Mirra. "They're getting bigger every year."

Mirra is one of the reasons for the soaring popularity of such alternative sports events as the X Games and the Gravity Games, as well as the skyrocketing sales of "extreme" merchandise. He's a sensational athlete, every bit as ambitious and accomplished as his counterparts in the NBA or NFL. And his fans know it. That's why they flock to see him on his annual tour. It's why they devour cereal and candy bearing his name and his stamp of approval. It's why they spend endless hours pretending they're Dave, whether flying on a BMX bike or in the relative safety of their home, at the controls of a video game.

Mirra's is just one of the stories you'll find on these pages. Stories of devotion and dedication, and, sometimes, disappointment. In the end, though, they are triumphant stories, featuring athletes who refused to give up on their dreams and who often have refused to play by the rules. You'll find snowboarders Ross Powers and Tara Dakides, short-track speed skater Apolo Ohno, freestyle motocross pioneer Mike Metzger, big-

● ●

**"Extreme sports are catching
up all over the world," observes
freestyle BMX legend Dave Mirra.
"They're getting bigger
every year."**

● ●

wave surfer Layne Beachley, and teen prodigies
Tori Allen (rock climbing) and Shaun White
(snowboarding and skateboarding).

They range in age from fourteen to almost thir-
ty. One of them grew up in Australia, another in
Africa. They are as different as the sports they
embrace. But they all have something in com-
mon: a desire to be the best and to live life to its
fullest.

Beats the alternative, wouldn't you say?

Tori ALLEN

DATE OF BIRTH: JULY 30, 1988

If you ever have the opportunity to meet Tori Allen, don't make the mistake of addressing her by her given name: Victoria. That sounds like the name of a figure skater or a ballerina, both of which she used to be. It is, as she likes to point out, "a prissy name."

But Tori…that's different. Tori sounds adventurous, strong, confident. A girl named Tori could be a rock climber, maybe the best in the world.

Although she hasn't quite ascended to that lofty height just yet, Tori has unquestionably made an impact on the sport of climbing. At only fourteen years of age she's already a three-time United States Competitive Climbing Association national champion. Not bad for a kid who isn't quite five feet tall and weighs only seventy-eight pounds. It's no wonder that so many people within the world of climbing consider Tori destined to become the sport's biggest star. No less an expert than Hans Florine, a world-class climber and two-time X Games gold medalist, says simply, "Tori has a shine to her."

That glow, along with Tori's fearlessness, can be traced back to her unique upbringing. The

• •

"I used to be a ballerina. I tried out for *The Nutcracker* once, and they told me, 'You would be a perfect Clara—except your arms are too muscular.' Man, that really made me mad."

• •

daughter of missionary parents, Tori traveled a lot when she was a little girl. As a toddler she lived in Europe. But in 1992 her parents accepted an assignment to a town in the West African country of Benin. It was there, Tori's parents have suggested, that she first became accustomed to being the object of attention and curiosity. "She

MONKEY MANIA

Tori not only climbs with a stuffed toy monkey attached to her harness, but also collects toy monkeys. She has over 200 of them! At competitions, she sometimes tosses out tiny monkey dolls to her fans! "Monkeys and I are a lot alike," Tori says. "We both have lots of energy and will climb until we're worn out. We rest, then climb again."

was the only white kid in a village of five thousand people," Tori's father, Steve Allen, told *Sports Illustrated*. "Everyone stared at her."

Like a lot of kids who don't quite fit in, Tori developed a special friendship with the family pet. This being Africa, however, her companion was neither a cat nor a dog, nor a fish nor a guinea pig.

"When I was six years old this guy came to our house with a baby monkey," Tori explained

during an online interview with **northface.com**. "He had killed its mother and he was selling the baby, which had no hair at all, for about five dollars. We bought him and named him Georgie."

For a while Georgie was Tori's best friend. The two were inseparable, and, in fact, Georgie was Tori's first climbing partner. He'd chase her up and down trees in the jungle surrounding the Allen home, scampering over branches and pushing her faster and higher, until the child became nearly as quick and agile as the monkey. Sadly, Georgie was bitten by a snake and died shortly before Tori's family returned to the United States in 1996.

"I cried for, like, two weeks straight," Tori

● ●

"The guy who was working the wall couldn't believe it. He said, 'Wow, you're really talented. You should get into this.'"

● ●

says. "So my dad bought a monkey stuffed animal for me when we got back home. I wear him on my climbing harness now as a reminder of Georgie and how special he was to me."

Despite her early fascination with climbing, Tori drifted into more traditional sports when she first settled in the United States. She danced and she skated. And she liked them both just fine. Until Christmas of 1997, when she visited a shopping mall in her hometown of Indianapolis and spotted a makeshift climbing wall. Then everything changed. Tori stood at the bottom of the wall and watched with wide eyes as a handful of instructors conducted clinics and exhibitions. After a while the little girl yanked on her father's sleeve.

"Please, Dad...can I try?"

While he wasn't exactly crazy about the idea of his nine-year-old daughter scaling a rock wall, Steve Allen figured he might as well just let her get it out of her system. It seemed reasonable to think that she'd get stuck halfway, become frustrated, lose interest, and go right back to figure skating. Imagine his surprise when Tori was suddenly transformed into Spiderman and crawled to the top of the wall on her very first try. Then she did it again...and again. Four times, on four different routes, Tori reached the top. Her father was shocked, and he wasn't alone.

"The guy who was working the wall couldn't believe it," Tori remembers. "He said, 'Wow, you're really talented. You should get into this.'"

When Tori woke up on Christmas morning she found a stack of brand-new climbing gear under the tree, along with a membership card to a local climbing gym. Within a month she had entered her first competition, a regional qualifier for the junior national championships. She took first place in that event. And while her talent may have been obvious, no one could have guessed that it would be the first of more than a dozen consecutive victories in the nineteen-and-under division. Or that Tori would begin beating grown women in open competitions. By the time she was eleven years old, Tori was one of the top sport climbers in the world.

With remarkably strong fingers and toes and unusually long arms, all sprouting off a thin, muscular body, Tori has the perfect physique for climbing. She also has the perfect support system. In fact, climbing has become a real family affair for the Allens. When Tori's gym ran into financial trouble a few years back, her parents bought the business and made it successful. They have since bought another rock climbing center. And when Tori trains, one of her partners is her

STAYING ON TRACK

One way Tori tries to stay fresh is by varying her training routine. In addition to climbing at least fifteen hours a week in the gym, she lifts weights to improve her strength. Tori also competes in the pole vault on her high school track team, even though she's usually the only girl in the event. She exercises her fingers by playing electric bass in her church band.

younger brother, Clark, who is also one of the best climbers in his age division.

"When we bought the gym, we didn't know the first thing about climbing," Steve Allen explains. "We just wanted to be with our kids."

Although Tori has tried many different types of climbing, her favorite is bouldering, in which competitors climb without ropes and leads, relying only on their strength and agility. Bouldering is done either on an indoor rock climbing wall or outside on boulders—rather than on sheer rock faces. Tori was only twelve years old when she became the American Bouldering Series women's national cochampion in 2001.

That accomplishment should have been

● ●

"I don't think. I just climb."

● ●

enough to last a year, if not a lifetime, but Tori immediately began looking for new challenges. As a student of the sport, Tori knows that "real" climbers are measured not only by the number of championships they win, but by the amount of time they spend outdoors. The smooth plastic of the gym is fine, but a real climber needs to test herself against nature once in a while. That's why Tori joined some of the top rock climbers in the world last year when they ascended the nose of El Capitan, a notoriously steep and craggy peak in Yosemite National Park. The trip took four days and left Tori exhausted but triumphant, as she became the youngest female in history to reach the summit!

With that achievement came a flood of sponsorship offers, but Tori is weighing her options carefully. In recent years there have been several American climbing prodigies who have burned out and retired before they were barely old enough to drive a car. Tori vows that won't happen to her.

"I love to compete," she says. "And I love the adrenaline rush of climbing."

That much is obvious. In August of 2002, Tori competed in the X Games for the very first time and turned in an awesome performance. The X Games has only one climbing event: speed climbing, in which competitors race up a 60-foot wall. Despite competing in only one previous speed climbing event, Tori stole the show. She not only won the gold medal, but also broke the X Games record by nearly four seconds! Not bad, considering she was nearly ten years younger than every other athlete in the competition. But Tori wasn't frightened.

"I was so happy just to compete, just to get anything," Tori said afterward. "I really just wanted to have fun."

Layne BEACHLEY

DATE OF BIRTH: MAY 24, 1972

When your name perfectly matches your sport, it can be both a blessing and a burden. Take Layne Beachley, for example. When she took up surfing as a kid in New South Wales, Australia, it seemed appropriate enough. But there were certain expectations. After all, if you have a name like "Beachley," you'd better not wipe out too often. It just wouldn't look right.

Fortunately, that hasn't been much of a problem for Layne, a fiercely competitive thirty-year-old who is widely regarded as the greatest female surfer in history. Whether chasing championship trophies or forty-foot swells in pursuit of the ultimate natural roller-coaster ride, Layne is as confident and capable as any woman who has ever set foot in the ocean. Or any man, for that matter.

"I love big waves," Layne says. "As a competitor, sometimes it scares the daylights out of me, but that's what makes it such an adrenaline rush."

Layne can scarcely recall a time when she wasn't involved in sports. Soccer and tennis were the first to draw her attention, and she excelled at both. But often, while biking to various athletic fields from her home in Sydney,

● ●

"With a big wave, the fear draws you to it and makes you respect it. You can't really attack it too much, because it attacks you right back."

● ●

she'd pass Manly Beach, a bustling surfer's paradise, and find herself mesmerized by the boards and the waves. One day she stopped and chatted with some of the surfers. Before long she was in the water, gliding along the crest of a wave. Just like that, Layne Beachley became a surfer. And Manly Beach became her second home. She would spend hours there, sometimes surfing, sometimes just walking and talking with other

surfers, picking up pointers from older, more experienced athletes. She was a bright, friendly girl who loved everything about the surfing scene, and she knew by the time she was in her early teens that her life would revolve around surfing.

Others soon figured it out, too, for Layne was an extremely gifted athlete. Her first taste of success came when she won a regional scholastic title in 1987, when she was a tenth grader at Mackellar Girls High School. With that performance Layne earned a spot in the New South Wales championships, and from there she went on to finish fifth in the Australian nationals. She was only fifteen years old, but already it was clear that Layne had the talent to be one of the best surfers in the world.

● ●

"When you're surfing, you can't pay attention to the people who are trying to direct you from the cliffs. You have to watch the waves. You have to watch the ocean and be directed by that."

● ●

Talent, however, is nothing without ambition and focus. Even as a teenager, Layne had both. Rather than spending the next few years slowly progressing through the amateur ranks (the route chosen by most surfers), she jumped straight into professional competition. Layne

was younger and smaller and far less experienced than most of her fellow competitors, but
she wasn't even slightly intimidated. She continued to train and improve. She worked harder
than anyone else on the pro surfing circuit. In
addition to spending hours in the water each
day, she ran and lifted weights. She embraced a
training regimen that left other surfers in awe of
her strength and endurance. And it all paid off.
By the time she was twenty years old, Layne was
no longer a skinny little kid. She was one of the
top-ranked surfers in the world. Her first World
Tour victory came in 1993, at the Diet Coke Surf
Classic in Australia.

"I had trained so hard for it that I knew I was
going to win," Layne recalls. "But it was still sort
of a shock. I was just relieved to have finally won
an event."

There would be many more victories, and a
growing reputation as a woman capable of tam-
ing the biggest of waves. But the 1990s were not
entirely pleasant for Layne. She struggled with
consistency. Some days she'd feel like there was
nothing she couldn't do on a surfboard. Other
days she felt like a beginner. Layne had always

DON'T BE SHY

Outgoing by nature, Layne has always taken every available opportunity to publicize herself, because she knows that no one else will do it for her. One Australian newspaper even labeled her "The Queen of Self-Promotion." In recent years Layne has occasionally moved to the other side of the microphone, working as a television reporter and commentator. She hopes to do more of that type of work after she retires from surfing.

been one of the most energetic and lively personalities in surfing, but by 1996 she had lost some of her enthusiasm. She'd wake up in the morning and have trouble getting out of bed. Many surfing observers had predicted that Layne would win several world championships, but by 1997, at the age of twenty-five, she was still searching for her first. She was even thinking about retirement.

Then everything suddenly changed. Layne saw a doctor who diagnosed her with chronic fatigue syndrome. Together they figured out a way to battle the illness, which often left Layne too exhausted to train. Then she met a fellow surfer named Ken Bradshaw, a big-wave specialist from Hawaii who became her boyfriend and training partner. By 1998 Layne was in the best shape of her life. She was a smoother and more consistent surfer. After finishing second to American Lisa Anderson in 1995 and 1997, Layne finally broke through and won her first overall world title in 1998. She was easily the most dominant woman on the tour that year, winning five of eleven tournaments and setting a record for the most prize money won by a woman in a single season. In fact, Layne earned more money that year than all but one of the male surfers on the pro tour!

"My shoulders sank to about my knees after I clinched the title," Layne says. "I was so relieved. Now I could claim myself as a world champion, rather than just talking about wanting to be one."

And that was only the beginning. Layne

repeated as overall world champion in 1999…and 2000…and 2001. As if that weren't enough, she began attacking some of the biggest and most dangerous waves on the planet. Big-wave surfing is an entirely different type of sport than competitive surfing. It's not about scoring and style and judging. It's not about medals and trophies and prize money. It's about something much more pure and primitive: the need to challenge nature. As *Transworld Surf* magazine said, "Layne Beachley is the only woman comfortable exploring the outer limits of modern surfing."

Accompanied by her husband and an adventurous surfing team known as the Billabong Odyssey, Layne traveled to Todos Santos Island off the coast of Mexico, in the spring of 2002. The group had one goal in mind: to find and ride the ocean's biggest waves. This was no small task. You don't just paddle out to these sorts of waves. You get pulled behind a boat at speeds that allow you to catch the wave without being blown over. And then you hang on for dear life. It's a sport few women have even attempted, but Layne displayed no hesitation. Bradshaw towed her into waves that measured fifty-five feet on the face (that's about the size of a five-story apartment building!), and from there Layne put on a remarkable show. More than a dozen times she rode into the massive waves, and each time she completed her ride without falling. The entire unforgettable performance was chronicled by a documentary film crew.

Wild About Waves

Layne's nickname on the pro surfing tour is Beast, a shortened version of Beastly, which, of course, sounds like her last name. The nickname has nothing to do with Layne's appearance and everything to do with her ferocious approach to surfing, where she routinely tames the toughest waves.

"Layne was just ripping today," observed Mike Parsons, part of the Billabong Odyssey crew. "There are very few men anywhere in the world who have ever ridden waves like she did out there today."

Layne has no intention of retiring from competitive surfing. She's still fit and eager to add more gold to her trophy case. And there is no reason to believe that she won't win several more world championships before she's through—as long as she can stay healthy. You see, there is a part of Layne that can't be satisfied by six-foot waves and the coziness of traditional tournaments. That's why she'll continue to test herself against nature's fury.

"As much as I love competing," she explains, "I have a need for speed. And that can only be fulfilled by riding big waves."

Tara DAKIDES

DATE OF BIRTH: AUGUST 20, 1975

Meet Tara Dakides, one of the most complex and compelling athletes in the world. With her long blond hair, bright green eyes, and delicate smile, she looks like she could be a model. And, in fact, she has been. Dig a little deeper, though, and you'll find a toughness and intensity unmatched in any sport. You'll find a young woman who once pierced her nose and naval, and who has a giant tattoo on her back. You'll find an unbreakable and driven athlete who has accumulated nearly as many broken bones and torn ligaments as she has X Games gold medals for snowboarding. And in the case of Tara, who has been to the top of the X Games podium five times, that's saying something.

"I'm not afraid of getting hurt," Tara explains matter-of-factly. "There are always going to be times when I eat dirt. It's part of the sport. I've fractured my back, dislocated elbows, torn up both my knees. I've gotten whiplash six or seven times and who knows how many concussions. This sport is all or nothing."

"This sport" is snowboarding, and no one has been better at it than Tara over the past five years. In addition to her dominance at the X Games, she's also captured three world championships, landed on the cover of numerous national magazines (not all of them devoted to snowboarding), and become an idol to young extreme sports fans across the country. One of

● ●

"I'll never get sick of winning. Besides, I don't always win, which is good. It's humbling."

● ●

the most interesting things about Tara is that young boys admire her not only because of her stunning good looks, but also because of her stunning athletic ability. Indeed, when Tara takes time out of her busy schedule for an online chat with fans, it's not unusual for her to juggle a wide range of interesting questions. For example, a technical question about how to perform a specific aerial maneuver might be followed closely by an invitation to a high school prom.

Tara, ever the gracious professional, handles them all with style and humility. For her, everything stems from her devotion to her sport.

"I ride because I love to snowboard," she told **EXPN.com**. "I guess I've kind of been placed in the position of being a role model, but that just came along with learning to snowboard."

Mammoth Pizza

Of all the bonuses that come with being a famous athlete, Tara says that perhaps the best is having a pizza joint name a pie after you. That's what a California restaurant in Mammoth Lakes has done, and it is, she admits with a laugh, "pretty cool."

Not that it's been easy. While it's true that Tara has a great deal of natural ability, no one has worked harder to achieve her success. She practices for hours on end, and she's notoriously tough on herself when trying to master a new trick. You need only to visit Tara when she's working out to understand that this is not some laid-back slacker. For Tara, it's not enough to simply make a pile of money in endorsements.

She's intensely competitive, and while she doesn't mind being complimented on her appearance, she also craves the respect that comes with being the best in her sport. To say she has earned that respect would be an understatement. In 2002 she was named women's rider of the year for the third time by *Snowboarder* magazine. The award was determined not by journalists or fans but rather by a vote of Tara's peers: other professional snowboarders.

One of the things that makes Tara special is her ability to cope with fear. She's not a reckless snowboarder, but she is willing to attempt tricks that others might consider a bit too dangerous. As a result, she's one of the very few females who soars as far and as high as the top male riders on the pro snowboarding circuit. Injuries, she says, are a small price to pay.

"I just see somebody do something, whether it be a girl or a guy, and I want to do it, too," she explains. "And if it scares me, then I just want to do it more. I don't like being scared, and I don't like thinking that I'm not going to do something just because I'm scared of it."

Tara learned at a relatively young age how to deal with fear and uncertainty. She was sixteen years old when her parents divorced and her life in

Mission Viejo, California, became suddenly chaotic. Confused and lonely, Tara dropped out of high school, sold her stereo system for three hundred dollars, and boarded a bus for the ski resort town of Mammoth Lakes, California. Tara had no real plan. She'd been snowboarding since she was thirteen, and she was already pretty good at it, thanks in part to her background in

• •

"When I'm on the mountain, I'm probably the furthest thing from feminine. But I also enjoy being a girl. There's nothing wrong with being an athlete and a beautiful woman."

• •

gymnastics and skateboarding. But she wasn't exactly ready for the professional circuit. She showed up in Mammoth Lakes with no job and only a handful of contacts. Despite the long odds, she was determined to create a new life for herself, one that revolved around something she loved: snowboarding. It was not a decision that made her parents happy.

"They supported me when I first started snowboarding," Tara remembers. "But when I got serious about it, and it started interfering

with school, and all the other things you're supposed to do, then they weren't so into it. They actually forbade me to snowboard. That didn't work very well. I just moved out. Now they're very supportive and proud. I don't hold it against them. It was a very parent thing to do. And who would have guessed that snowboarding would get so huge so fast?"

By her own admission, Tara was lucky. She

A VERSATILE ATHLETE

While snowboarding is clearly Tara's specialty, it is not her only sport. In 1997 she won several motocross events, and she's also a talented and daring surfer who has ridden some of the biggest waves in the world.

made friends quickly, landed a part-time job, and spent endless hours on the slopes, refining her snowboarding technique. Before long, people began to take notice. Tara was offered a few small sponsorship deals. The money wasn't great, but it helped cover some of her living expenses and boosted her reputation as an athlete with a future.

If she could stay healthy, that is.

The serious injuries started in 1993, less than a year after Tara arrived in Mammoth Lakes, when a torn knee ligament cost her five months of training. The following year, while attempting a backflip for the first time (no woman had ever successfully executed that trick), she suffered a broken vertebra in her back. That injury was nearly catastrophic. It could have left Tara paralyzed. But she didn't slow down and she didn't lose confidence, not even when she was dropped by one of her primary sponsors in 1996. Instead, Tara worked even harder. She was determined to be one of the best snowboarders in the world, and she was willing to risk everything to achieve that goal, including her body.

Tara's perseverance paid off in 1998, when she became the first woman to land a backflip in competition. It happened at the big-air finals of the Vans Triple Crown, and the impact was felt almost immediately throughout the snowboarding world.

"A bunch of us guys were watching the women's contest on a television monitor," Tara's boyfriend, snowboarder Kevin Jones, told *Sports Illustrated*. "I knew she'd been consistently hitting flips in practice, but when it happened on the screen, everyone went wild. She'd made her mark, and we all knew it."

Since that day, there's been no looking back for Tara. She's won six X Games medals, all but one of them gold. Most recently she took home the gold medal in slopestyle at the 2002 Winter X Games in Aspen, Colorado. Along the way she's become not only the biggest star in snowboarding, but a young woman whose crossover appeal has made her one of the hottest athletes of her generation. Hard to believe? Well, consider this: in 2001, when *Sports Illustrated for Women* selected its "Coolest Girls in Sports," Tara was profiled

• •

"I'm not afraid of getting hurt. There are always going to be times when I eat dirt. It's part of the sport. I've fractured my back, dislocated elbows, torn up both my knees. This sport is all or nothing."

• •

right alongside such acknowledged superstars as WNBA guard Teresa Witherspoon and tennis champion Serena Williams. In fact, guess whose smiling face was featured on the cover? That's right—Tara Dakides!

"I can't believe they would choose me for the cover," Tara said when the magazine was published. "I mean, these women are so awesome. Why me?"

That's a question that doesn't really need answering, isn't it?

Mike METZGER

DATE OF BIRTH: NOVEMBER 19, 1975

Mike Metzger just can't resist a challenge. That's why the man known as the Godfather of Freestyle Motocross was out in the backyard of his home in Meniffee, California, on July 2, 2002, roaring around his private course, preparing to attempt something that was once thought impossible. With a small crowd watching and video cameras recording the event, Mike hit the throttle and guided his dirt bike to the top of a ramp. He soared high into the air and over a gap that stretched nearly fifty feet. And then he landed safely.

All of that sounds impressive enough, but it's really nothing new for Mike or any other freestyle motocross rider. It's what happened

along the way that set Mike apart and estab-
lished a new standard for the sport. In midair he
pulled back on the handlebars of his 210-pound
motorcycle and launched into a backflip. No one
had ever successfully executed that maneuver,
and only a handful had even attempted it. The
few who had tried it suffered serious injuries.

● ●

**"My goal is to live a happy,
healthy, and successful life. And
to be able to take care of my
family in return for what they did
for me when I was growing up.
My mom and dad have situated
me in a career where I couldn't
ask for any more fun."**

● ●

But Mike has never been one to worry about the
consequences of his sport, which can be both
fun and extremely dangerous. As he once told
Dirt Rider magazine, "Nothing really scares me. I
think I've proven that fact over and over as far as
trying to step up my sport or my life to the next
level."

The biggest challenge to landing a backflip is

maintaining control of the bike. It's simply too heavy and powerful. Most riders who have tried the trick end up letting go and plummeting to earth. Then, if they're lucky, they limp away. Others get carried off on a stretcher. But not Mike. He used his strength to yank the bike backward, and he hung on for dear life. The bike rotated perfectly and hit the ground smoothly, with the rider still on board. Mike raised his arms in triumph and waved to the cameras and the small crowd.

Then he did it all over again. Before the practice session was over, Mike had successfully completed the backflip five times. And he didn't even have a bruise to show for it.

"I knew I could do it," Mike said afterward. "I've been practicing it on my BMX bike, and I was sure I could do it on my dirt bike. I'm just so happy. The Godfather is back!"

Not that he's ever really been away. At twenty-six years of age, in a sport dominated by teens, Mike is something of an old-timer. When he was pioneering the sport of freestyle back in the mid-1990s, many current riders were still in grade school. But he's lost none of his competitive fire, as the backflip surely proved. Among the spectators who witnessed this epic achievement was Paul Taublieb, president of Moto-X Co., which organizes freestyle motocross for the Summer X Games.

"Metzger did what was said couldn't be

done," Taublieb told **EXPN.com**. "A full, floating backflip over a big gap. This sport is constantly progressing, and the backflip is almost a metaphor for the sport itself. Other riders have cracked the door open a bit and deserve props. But fittingly, the man credited for starting the entire freestyle movement, Mike Metzger, busted the door down and sent the sport hurtling into the future. There is no looking back now."

True enough. But to understand the future of freestyle motocross, you have to know a little about the past…and the past of the man who helped get it started. Freestyle motocross is the adventurous offspring of traditional motocross. The term "freestyle" was used to describe the entertaining tricks and jumps performed by riders who had fallen far behind in a race and thus had nothing left to lose. Some of these maneuvers were so popular with fans that they actually diverted interest from the race itself. This led to separate competitions for freestyle riders, complete with spectators, loud music, and a panel of judges.

"Everyone tells me I started the sport," Mike

A FAN'S NOTES

Mike is a serious competitor, but he also admires several other freestyle riders, most notably eighteen-year-old X Games sensation Travis Pastrana. "He's the friendliest rider out there," Mike says of Travis. "But he also loves to ride and kick everyone's butt. I love to watch him ride."

says. "I guess that's because when I was younger and racing, I was more worried about being the fastest one over a jump rather than worrying about turns. I've always had more fun jumping my dirt bike rather than practicing lap after lap."

The first official freestyle motocross events were held in 1998, and Mike was at the forefront of the movement. The new sport was perfectly suited to Mike, who had been born into a racing family (his father raced dirt bikes before a back injury ended his career) and started riding minibikes when he was barely old enough to walk. By the time he was a teenager, Mike had graduated to motorcycles. He was a competitive

Portrait of the Artist

Mike is not just a motorcycle rider. He's also a talented artist whose creativity can be seen in the tattoos he designs and the paintings he creates.

racer throughout much of the 1990s, and while he did have a fair amount of success, he never challenged for a title. In fact, Mike was usually happy if he finished among the top twenty riders at the motocross nationals.

But Mike was always one of the most daring and innovative of riders. He did tricks during races. He put on jumping exhibitions for the fans. And they loved him for it! Mike's exploits were so dramatic that he wound up getting a lot of coverage from the motocross press—even more than riders who usually beat him in races. When freestyle motocross went mainstream, Mike was ready to seize the opportunity. He instantly became the biggest star in the sport, winning the Vans Triple Crown championship in both 1998 and 1999. Since then he has helped make freestyle motocross one of the most popular events at such alternative sports festivals as the X Games and Gravity Games.

"The best part of freestyle is that there's really no pressure," Mike told *Dirt Rider*. "I never put any pressure on myself to go out and do a great two-minute run for a final. Basically, the way I get pumped up is by giving my family some hugs and telling them I'll see them after the two minutes are over—after I win. I just love being able to win in front of my family, and I love pumping it up for the crowd."

● ●

"My words of wisdom for kids? If you have a goal in life, set your mind on it and get it done. Don't give up on your goals until they're old news, until you've already accomplished them and decided it's time to move on to something else."

● ●

As much as Mike loves freestyle motocross, he knows that he won't be able to compete forever. He's already far beyond what most people would consider to be the prime age. That's why he's putting more time into running his own business, which includes a web site and motocross store. You see, freestyle motocross has a way of inflicting pain and punishment on almost all of its participants. Mike is no exception. By his own conservative estimate, he's suffered twenty broken bones.

"Big bones," he hastens to add. "Legs, arms. Things like that. That's not including little injuries, like broken fingers and toes, stitches in my head and knees."

Although he has the respect and admiration of his peers and is generally acknowledged to be one of the best riders in the history of freestyle motocross, Mike has never won a medal at the X Games. Since freestyle was added to the X Games lineup in 1999, injuries have prevented him from competing at his best. He suffered a nasty injury at the 2000 Gravity Games, where he fractured a vertebra and shattered both of his heels. After falling on his face during a practice run at the X Games, he wound up back on the sidelines.

"Not very smart," Mike admits. "I wasn't ready to start jumping again. I should have just watched [the X Games] and allowed myself to heal instead of hurting myself worse."

• •

"Everyone tells me I started the sport," Mike says. "I guess that's because when I was younger and racing, I was more worried about being the fastest one over a jump rather than worrying about turns. I've always had more fun jumping my dirt bike rather than practicing lap after lap."

• •

As Mike knows, however, freestyle isn't the only type of motocross in which riders get hurt. In fact, in his last year of racing, Mike suffered two broken legs and third-degree burns on his back. More recently, while training for a return to motocross racing, he slammed his face into the frame of his bike. Sixteen stitches closed the wounds on his chin and cheek, but the five broken teeth he suffered required a bit more time to heal. Typically, though, Mike was back on his bike the very next day.

"It's awesome being able to ride," Mike explains. "Whether it's freestyle, racing, or whatever. I just enjoy it. So even though I've been hurt really bad sometimes, I just can't seem to get away from the bike. I know I won't be able to jump forever, but hopefully as long as I can walk, I can ride motorcycles."

Dave MIRRA

DATE OF BIRTH: APRIL 4, 1974

They call Dave Mirra "Miracle Boy." Why? Well, because the things he can do on a bicycle sometimes seem almost impossible. This is a guy who has been riding professionally for sixteen years now. He ought to be thinking about retiring. And yet somehow he just continues to improve. An innovator as well as a competitor, Dave has won ten gold medals (thirteen overall!) at the Summer X Games. No one else has come close to matching his success at the world's biggest extreme sports festival.

Miracle Boy? Sure, why not, although Miracle Man would be more appropriate at this point. And if you want further evidence that Dave is really something special, just take a trip back in time to 1993, when he suffered the most serious injury of his life. This one didn't happen on a vert ramp or a street course. It didn't even happen on a bicycle. Dave was just minding his own business, walking across the street, when he was run down by a drunk driver. The impact left Dave with a fractured skull and a potentially fatal blood clot on his brain. Fortunately, doctors

• •

"When I see my tricks on video, it's kind of weird. They always look a lot harder than they feel."

• •

were able to save his life, but they warned him that the injury could have a lasting effect on his balance and vision. They strongly advised him against ever riding again.

But Dave couldn't imagine life without his bike. He was nineteen years old at the time and already one of the most promising stunt riders in the world. He wasn't about to quit. So Dave let his mind and body heal. After many months, he eventually felt strong enough to resume training. Less than a year after nearly losing his life, Dave was back in the saddle.

"I believe everything happens for a reason,"

Dave told the *New Straits Times*. I'm still the same person I was back then, before the accident. Only now, I feel lucky with what I've achieved. I'm glad to be here and to be able to participate in the sport."

The most decorated competitor in the history of freestyle BMX was born and raised in Chittenango, New York, near Syracuse. Despite

Don't Drink and Drive

The accident that nearly cost Dave his life has left him with a strong attitude about drinking and driving. Although he hasn't done any public service announcements, Dave says, "It's my stand that drinking and driving is not safe and I would urge people not to drink and drive. It's just not worth it."

growing up in the snowbelt of the Northeast, where winter can stretch across seven months of the year, Dave logged plenty of time on his bike. He learned how to ride when he was only four years old, and by five had already adopted the attitude and spirit of a stunt rider. It wasn't at all unusual even then to see Dave, a tiny boy in a helmet and pads, jumping over curbs in his neighborhood and flying off makeshift dirt

ramps in his backyard.

Like most kids, Dave was interested in a lot of different sports when he was younger. He liked basketball and tennis, and he was pretty good at both of them. Even when Dave entered his first freestyle BMX contest, at the age of ten, he had no idea that he had any sort of special ability. That event was held in Columbus, Ohio, and Dave's performance was hardly the stuff of legend. He rode badly and finished next-to-last. But you know what? He didn't really care. Dave just enjoyed riding, and so he kept at it. After a while he discovered that he liked riding on vert ramps best of all, so that's where he devoted most of his time and energy. He continued to compete, and before long his trophy case was clogged with hardware. Sponsors and promoters naturally began to take notice. Dave was only thirteen years old when he signed his first endorsement contract. At that point Dave knew he had a chance to be one of the better athletes in the new and evolving sport of freestyle BMX. By the time he graduated from high school, Dave was already ranked among the world's best freestyle riders.

And then came the accident and the one-year break from training and competition. But Dave came back stronger and more determined than ever. When the Summer X Games debuted, giving Dave and other alternative sports athletes a bigger stage on which to perform, he became practically a household name. Dave made his first X Games appearance in 1996 and instantly became one of the event's biggest stars. He surprised a lot of people that summer, not just because he rode flawlessly, but because he won both the street and vert titles. In an age of specialization, Dave seemed to be a master of all forms of bicycle stunt riding. By 1999, however, after he'd swept both events for the fourth con-

• •

"I don't play a lot of computer games, but I play mine. It gives me a break from the real thing."

• •

secutive year, such versatility and excellence were expected of Dave. He was the undisputed king of freestyle BMX, an athlete who rode for the pure joy of it, but who also thrived on competition. The bigger the event, the better Dave seemed to perform.

"Dave rules!" observes Jay Miron, another top freestyle BMX rider. "He steps it up when it counts."

No doubt about that. Dave could have rode off into the sunset after his fourth double in 1999, but instead he continued to develop new and even more impressive tricks. In 2000 he

won a gold medal in street at the X Games and a silver in vert. Then, just one month later, he won a gold medal in vert at the Gravity Games. The following year was equally impressive. In addition to entertaining thousands of fans across the country with the Dave Mirra BMX Supertour, Dave won a record twelfth gold medal (in vert)

• •

"Dave rules!" observes Jay Miron, another top freestyle BMX rider. "He steps it up when it counts."

• •

at the X Games, and was BMX Rider of the Year at the ESPN Action Sports & Music Awards.

"The tours and road trips are a lot of fun because you get to be out there with your friends," Dave told **EXPN.com**. "The X Games and Gravity Games I look forward to in a different sense. That's a lot tougher. There's plenty of pressure on your shoulders and you have to try to ride your best. Sometimes it doesn't work out, but you just have to keep a positive attitude and be prepared."

Neither of those things has ever been much of a problem for Dave, who is considered one of

NO TIME TO RELAX

Dave's business obligations take up a lot of his time now, but he still trains as hard as he ever did. He works out at least three hours each day. As Dave knows, there are no shortcuts. "You can't put off training or practice," he says.

the most professional and polite athletes in alternative sports. In addition to being a talented rider, Dave is a smart businessman who has built a small empire. He has lucrative endorsement deals with companies such as Adidas and Haro Bikes. He's also lent his name and expertise to a series of video games that have become some of the biggest sellers in history. There are Dave Mirra trading cards, Dave Mirra bubble gum, and Dave Mirra action figures. In other words, there's a lot of money to be made in the marketing of Miracle Boy. Dave understands that his good fortune stems mostly from his ability to invent and execute remarkable tricks on a bike. But he also knows that without the support of his fans, none of this would be possible. So he treats them at all times with respect. The BMX Supertour, where fans get a chance to chat with Dave and other top riders, is a perfect example.

"My life is still at a point where I find it flattering when fans come up to me and want my autograph," he says. "I think it's important to give something back to the sport."

Apolo OHNO

DATE OF BIRTH: MAY 22, 1982

When you watch Apolo Anton Ohno on the ice today, he's so smooth and strong. With his long hair flowing from beneath his helmet and his soul patch of beard highlighting his face, he looks every inch the Olympic superstar. In fact, it's almost impossible to imagine Apolo as anything less than the greatest short-track speed skater in the world.

But nothing is ever as simple as it appears. The truth is, there was a time when Apolo struggled with anxiety and self-doubt. He wondered whether he'd ever amount to anything as an athlete.

"I always knew I had potential," Apolo says. "But I was kind of immature. And I was rebellious."

If Apolo lacked direction, it's probably because he had an unusual and often difficult childhood. As a result, it took time for him to harness his immense physical gifts. Everything worked out in the end, of course—Apolo emerged from the 2002 Winter Olympics as one of the most popular and successful athletes on the planet. But the road from Seattle, Washington, where he was born, to Salt Lake City, Utah, where he struck Olympic gold, was long and frequently bumpy.

• •

"Speed skating is like floating on ice. When I'm in a great mood and my spirits are light, it's just a beautiful feeling. It's like I'm gliding."

• •

Most people assume that Apolo is named after the Greek god Apollo, but that's not the case at all. While it's true that his first name is Greek, it actually comes from the words "ap," meaning "to lead," and "lo," which means "away from." His last name is Japanese. The translation for Ohno is "large field." So Apolo Ohno's name means "to lead away from a large field." Considering what Apolo has accomplished and how often he leaves other competitors behind, it seems like the perfect name. But Yuki Ohno,

Apolo's father, had no intention of raising an Olympic champion. He just wanted his son to be happy. That alone was enough of a challenge.

Yuki was a young hairdresser who had emigrated from Japan and opened his own salon when Apolo was born. Less than a year later, Yuki and his wife divorced, and Apolo's mother moved away, leaving Yuki to raise the child on his own. Apolo has never spoken to his mother, and while he never expresses any anger about her absence from his life, he always makes a point of thanking his father publicly.

"My father has always been the strongest influence in my life," Apolo says. "He's one of the hardest-working people I've ever known. I respect him in so many ways."

Yuki and Apolo are the closest of friends today, but like many fathers and sons, they went through some hard times. Yuki was a young and inexperienced father trying hard to establish a career and support a family. Apolo was often left with baby-sitters. Sometimes he'd hang out for hours on end at Yuki's hair salon, playing with the equipment and driving the customers crazy with his boundless energy. Yuki's parenting philosophy was simple: try to keep Apolo so busy that he'd be exhausted at the end of the day.

Apolo took swimming lessons. He learned how to roller-skate. He even sang in the school choir.

Apolo was only twelve years old when it became apparent that he was a uniquely talented athlete. That's when he won a state title in swimming. Two years later he won a national in-line skating championship. There was just one problem: Apolo wasn't training very hard. He

was content to get by on natural ability. At the same time, he began hanging out with some bad kids. A few of his friends ended up getting arrested and spending time in jail. That never happened to Apolo, but he did get in trouble. He skipped school. He stayed out all night. It seemed like he was on the verge of wasting his enormous potential.

Until he discovered short-track speed skating.

Apolo had become fascinated with the sport in 1994, after watching the Winter Olympic Games on television. Short track was faster and more exciting than traditional speed skating.

Contact Sport

Short-track speed skating is one of the roughest of winter sports. Although intentional pushing or shoving is forbidden, contact is unavoidable, especially when you're skating at thirty-five miles per hour. As Apolo notes, "Sometimes you just can't help it. There's bound to be some bumping."

Apolo liked the physical nature of the sport, the way the athletes used their elbows and hands to maneuver for position. People were always bumping and falling and crashing in short track. To an energetic thirteen-year-old boy, it looked like the greatest sport in the world.

Apolo's athleticism, combined with his experience as an in-line skater, allowed him to make rapid progress as a short-track speed skater. Within a year he was one of the country's best skaters in his age group. That success opened doors for Apolo. In the spring of 1995 he became the youngest athlete ever invited to the United States Olympic Training Center in Lake Placid, New York. It was a great opportunity. In Lake Placid, Apolo would have access to some of the best coaching and training facilities in the world. There was just one problem: He didn't really want to leave home. The idea of training five or six hours a day didn't appeal to Apolo. He was not that dedicated. Not yet. In fact, when Yuki drove Apolo to the airport in June of 1996, just a few weeks after the boy's fourteenth birthday, Apolo had an escape all planned out. He waved good-bye to his father, waited a few minutes, and then called a friend for a ride. Several weeks passed before he returned home.

"My father was pretty angry," Apolo recalled in an interview with **usolympicteam.com**. "But I was so young. And I was against any kind of authority."

Yuki didn't give up. One month later he made another trip to the airport, and this time

NO DISTRACTIONS

After his disappointing performance at the 1998 Olympic trials, Apolo decided to clear his mind by spending a week alone at a cabin on the coast of Washington State. He had no phone, no television, no radio, no car. Most of his time was spent walking or running on the beach, trying to figure out how he could accomplish his goal of becoming an Olympic champion. Obviously, he found the right answer.

Apolo didn't get away. In fact, Yuki flew to Lake Placid with him. Apolo did not adjust quickly or easily to his new home. He was a big-city kid suddenly living in the mountains, and he didn't like it at all. Nor did he like the difficult work-outs that consumed most of each day. Apolo was so angry that he didn't even attempt to fit in. He didn't try his hardest when he skated. On long training runs, sometimes he'd deliberately fall far off the pace and then duck out for a couple slices of pizza. Secretly he hoped that if he behaved badly enough, maybe the center's coaches would send him back home.

"I hated it there," Apolo told *Sports Illustrated*. "I didn't want anybody to help me."

Apolo's attitude changed late that summer, mainly because of embarrassment. When all of the speed skaters at the training center were tested to see what kind of shape they were in, Apolo's score was the worst. He was so fat and out of shape that it seemed like he finally deserved the nickname that his friends had given him when he was eight years old: Chunky. Apolo's pride was badly damaged, but once he made up his mind to get serious about speed skating, everything began to fall into place. Instead of finishing last in training runs, he finished first. On the ice, he was unbeatable.

"He totally changed," remembers Patrick Wentland, his coach at the time. "I'd never seen that kind of turnaround so fast."

By the time he was fifteen years old, Apolo had captured his first national title. But he suffered another setback in 1998, when he failed to qualify for the U.S. Olympic team. That disappointment led Apolo to train even harder. He won his first world junior title in 1999, at the age of seventeen, and the World Cup overall championship in 2001. Because he was such a powerful and versatile skater, many observers thought he had a chance to win four gold medals at the 2002 Olympics. He had a chance to make history.

• •

"In short track, you can't ever take a race for granted until you cross the finish line."

• •

But Apolo knew the odds were against him. Short track is a wild and unpredictable sport. To win, you not only have to be fast and courageous, but a little bit lucky as well. In his first event, the 1,000 meters, fate wasn't on Apolo's side. On the final lap, just as he surged into the lead, Apolo got caught in a crash that left four of the race's six competitors flat on their backs. He managed to slide across the line in second place, which was a tremendous accomplishment. A few minutes later, however, he discovered that he'd cut his thigh in the accident. Apolo didn't complain. After taking six stitches to close the wound, he climbed the awards platform and happily accepted his silver medal.

Three nights later it was Apolo's turn to catch a lucky break. He was awarded the gold medal in the 1,500 meters after being illegally cut off by a South Korean skater in the homestretch. His victory was the first by an American male in short-track speed skating!

"They can bury me in the desert now," Apolo said afterward with a big smile. "I've got my gold medal."

Ross POWERS

DATE OF BIRTH: FEBRUARY 10, 1979

At first glance, Ross Powers seems like the grand old man of snowboarding. After all, this is a guy who has been competing for nearly fifteen years. He's won two Olympic medals, including one gold, and a backpack full of trophies in other international events, most notably the X Games and Gravity Games. He runs his own snowboarding camp and has a long list of lucrative endorsement contracts. In short, he's one of the most successful athletes ever to strap on a snowboard.

But you know which line on Ross's résumé is the most impressive? The one that reveals his age. You see, despite having accumulated a lifetime of accomplishments, Ross is still a very young man. In fact, at twenty-four years old, he's at an age when many athletes would just be

starting their professional careers. And yet, unlike most of his fellow competitors, Ross can vividly recall a time when snowboarding wasn't nearly the mainstream sport it is today.

"I think the Olympics changed a lot of people's minds about snowboarding," Ross said in an interview with **usolympicteam.com** "They could see that we're athletes trying as hard as anybody. When I first started out it was just a bunch of skateboarders on snow. Now when I go out to a hill I see entire families getting involved in the sport. A few years ago you'd go out to a mountain and there would be only one snowboarding trail, and it would always be way off to the side, or at the top. Now you can go to that same mountain and the trail is right where the main lift is."

● ●

"Ever since I was a kid, I just wanted to be on snow."

● ●

It's no exaggeration to suggest that Ross and snowboarding grew up together. Ross and his younger brother were raised in Londonderry, Vermont, by a single mother who had a job at nearby Bromley Mountain. Like any kid who spent a lot of time around a winter resort, Ross started skiing early (when he was just a toddler) and became proficient at a young age. He liked the speed and excitement of skiing, and most of his friends and family thought one day he might become a serious competitor. But when a friend stopped by his house one day with something that looked like a cross between a surfboard and a skateboard, Ross chucked his skis into the closet. They've been there ever since.

"I don't think we even called it a snowboard," Ross recalls. "It was blue and made out of wood, and it had little rubber bindings. A really early model. We used it to cruise down the hill behind my house."

• •

"I think snowboarding is a safe sport. Unfortunately, some kids play snowboarding video games and think they can go out there and do the same thing. And they can't. But if you take your time, learn, and have good equipment, snowboarding is pretty safe."

• •

Ross was only six years old at the time. Over the course of the next few months, snowboards began appearing with some regularity at Bromley Mountain, although it seemed like the only people courageous enough to give the sport a try were the lift attendants. Ross loved to stand at the bottom of the mountain and watch the young men cut through the snow on their boards.

"It looked so cool," he says. "It was so new,

and so totally different."

Money was usually in short supply in the Powers household, but Ross remembers that Christmas as being one of the best, mainly because he received a brand-new snowboard. "I didn't even care about the rest of my presents," Ross says. "I just ran right outside and took a couple runs in the backyard."

Ross quickly became infatuated with snowboarding. It grabbed his attention in a way that skiing never had. Bromley Mountain became his second home. After school he'd jump off the bus, run into the house, grab his board, and head for the mountain. Even on weekends, while his mom worked, Ross would spend almost every waking moment at Bromley, inventing and perfecting new tricks and jumps.

"Snowboarding was my baby-sitter," Ross often jokes. But he really isn't kidding. "Some days I'd be out on the slopes from eight in the morning until five in the afternoon, hanging with whoever was there, usually older kids who were into the sport."

Ross got a taste of big-time competition early. He was only in fourth grade when he received an invitation to take part in the U.S. Open at Stratton Mountain.

"Back then there weren't too many snow-boarders," he says. "And it wasn't like I was in the main event. They had qualifiers in the morning and finals in the afternoon. Still, I was in the U.S. Open, and for me it was awesome. My teacher was super cool about it, too. She worked at Stratton on the weekends, and she was into snowboarding, so she brought the whole class up to watch."

Although he liked the creativity involved in freestyle snowboarding, Ross concentrated on racing for several years. It wasn't until he entered a halfpipe competition at the United States Ski and Snowboard Association Nationals that his career took a dramatic turn. Ross was only fourteen years old at the time and still something of a novice on the halfpipe. So he didn't anticipate making much of an impact in the event. But guess what? Ross took first place! Shortly thereafter he was offered a spot on the U.S. national snowboarding team.

Even now there are times when Ross says he misses the pure competition of racing. But it sure seems like he made the right choice. At 5 feet, 9 inches, and 175 pounds, with a background in gymnastics and skateboarding as well as skiing, Ross is a strong and acrobatic freestyle snow-

MOTHER'S DAY

When Ross won his Olympic gold medal, he was quick to thank the people who have helped him along the way, most notably his mother: "My mom worked all the time to take care of me and my brother. She spent a lot of money so that I could compete and have the right equipment. If it wasn't for her, none of this would have been possible."

boarder. In the past few years, no one has collected more titles and trophies. In 1998, for example, Ross won a pair of gold medals at the Winter X Games, in addition to a bronze medal at the first Olympic snowboarding competition. The following year he was the U.S. Open halfpipe champion, and in 2000 he earned gold medals at the Gravity Games and Goodwill Games and was the world halfpipe champion.

"There was a time when everyone wanted to be the best all-around, but these days that's almost impossible," Ross says of his decision to give up racing and concentrate exclusively on freestyle. "It's just too competitive. There's almost no one who does well in both racing and pipe."

If there was any doubt that Ross was king of the halfpipe, it was laid to rest in February of 2002, at the Winter Olympics in Salt Lake City, Utah. Competing on a "superpipe" nearly seventeen feet high, in front of a raucous crowd of more than 30,000 spectators (and a worldwide television audience of several hundred million), Ross turned in the performance of his life. He nailed his first jump and received the highest score of the day to lead an American sweep of the top three spots. Just one day after his twenty-third birthday, Ross was an Olympic gold medalist!

"I couldn't ask for anything more," he said after accepting his award. "It's the best birthday present ever. Today was just the perfect day."

In the days and weeks that followed his Olympic triumph, Ross became an international celebrity. But in a sport known for producing and rewarding outrageous personalities, he remains soft-spoken and humble. He still lives in Vermont, not far from where he grew up. And, in fact, all of the proceeds from his snowboarding camp are donated to the Ross Powers Foundation, which provides financial assistance and training to prom-

BORED WITH BOARDING? NOT LIKELY

Even when Ross stops competing, he can't imagine that he'll ever retire completely from snowboarding. He simply loves the sport too much. "There are some people in our sport who just go out to cool places and hit jumps and take good photos and videos," he says. "When contests get kind of old to me, I'd like to do some of that."

ising young Vermont athletes.

As for his personal goals, Ross just wants to keep improving. He hopes to win a few more X Games medals and perhaps even another gold at the 2004 Winter Olympics in Italy. Don't count him out. He'll only be twenty-six.

Shaun WHITE

DATE OF BIRTH: SEPTEMBER 4, 1986

How's this for a fantasy?

You're fifteen years old. One day the phone rings, and on the other end is Tony Hawk, skateboarding legend, multimillionaire entrepreneur, and all-around good guy. He tells you he's putting together another of his famous summer barnstorming tours, featuring many of the best extreme sports athletes in the world. He tells you he admires your skating. You thank him. And then he does something you never imagined, something out of a dream: He invites you to join the tour.

For Shaun White, this was no fantasy. He spent the better part of a month in the summer of 2002 on Hawk's Boom Boom Huckjam Tour, hanging out with the king of alternative sports, learning from the master.

"I was just so stoked when Tony asked me to go," Shaun says. "He's been a huge influence on my life. I've learned a lot of tricks, and I've learned about the business from him, because he's been through everything I'm going through right now."

●●●●●●●●●●●●●●●●●●●●●●●●●●●●●●●

"I never thought that just snow-boarding and having fun would get me into a video game."

●●●●●●●●●●●●●●●●●●●●●●●●●●●●●●●

Well, not quite. While it's true that Tony was a trailblazer some twenty years ago, inventing skateboarding tricks that remain popular today, he was actually less of a prodigy than Shaun White. You see, even though Shaun is one of the most promising and exciting young skateboarders in the world, skating isn't even his best sport. Snowboarding is.

"Shaun is amazing," observes Ross Powers, who won a gold medal in snowboarding at the 2002 Winter Olympics. "For his age, I just can't believe how consistent and smooth he is. He's such a natural."

Terje Haakonsen, who is to snowboarding what Hawk is to skateboarding—a legend—puts it another way: "Shaun is scary."

Maybe he was destined to be this way.

Certainly there's no denying that Shaun has the genes to be an extreme sports superstar. Many years ago his grandparents raced on the professional Roller Derby circuit! And just about everyone in his family seems to have a passion for skiing and snowboarding. His older brother, Jesse, is also a professional snowboarder, and his sister, Kari, won the junior halfpipe title at the 2000 U.S. Open. Mom and Dad are snowboarders, too. So, while some kids might have a hard time convincing their parents that

Knock on Wood

Despite his aggressive and acrobatic style, Shaun has never been seriously hurt while snowboarding. In fact, his most serious injuries came in a skateboarding accident a few years ago at the MTV Sport and Music Fest in Texas. Shaun collided with another skater and suffered a fractured skull and broken bones in his hand and foot.

snowboarding is a safe and reasonable hobby (or even a career), Shaun never had that problem. As he wrote on his internet web site, "I feel really lucky to have a family that snowboards and is as close as mine."

Shaun was only six years old the first time he tried snowboarding. It happened on a family skiing trip to June Mountain in California. Shaun watched Jesse race down the slope, and rather than finding it frightening, he thought snowboarding looked like the greatest sport in the world.

"I just thought it seemed really cool, a lot of fun," Shaun recalls. "So I started, too. I'd already been skateboarding for a while, so I knew a little bit about balance, which helped."

Despite the fact that he grew up near San Diego, California, more than three hours from the closest ski resort and six hours from the closest halfpipe, Shaun developed quickly as a snowboarder. San Diego was a haven for skateboarders (that's where Tony Hawk grew up, too), so Shaun had already logged countless hours at skate parks, refining his technique and testing his courage. All that practice proved valuable whenever Shaun's family went off to the mountains to ski and snowboard.

Within a few months he had entered his first snowboarding contest, and it wasn't long before he began piling up trophies and ribbons. Shaun was only eight years old in 1994 when he won his first United States of America Snowboard Association overall amateur title. The following year, at the 1995 U.S. Open, Shaun put on an exhibition that practically stole the show from the older, more experienced professional riders.

"We'd have little kids warm up the crowd and let them know that the serious stuff was about to happen," remembers Jake Burton Carpenter, the founder of Burton Snowboards and a pioneer of the sport. "This time was dif-

• •

"I put a lot of pressure on myself. I'm always trying to push the level of my riding."

• •

ferent. Simply put, Shaun went off! The whole experience reminded me of going to a concert where the warm-up act leaves more of an impression than the band you went to see."

Needless to say, it wasn't long afterward that Shaun began riding for Burton. Other sponsorships have followed, and today, despite his youth, Shaun is one of the hottest commercial prospects in alternative sports. And his life has been anything but ordinary. Shaun attends a public high school when he's home, but he travels so frequently that much of his course work is completed through independent study. He turned professional in 1998, after winning his fifth amateur championship. Ever since

WORLD TRAVELER

Shaun is no accidental tourist. He's an adventurous traveler who likes to soak up the culture of each country he visits. He's especially daring when it comes to food, although even Sean has his limits. "I love Japanese food," he says. "Especially sushi. But some of the stuff over there is just too crazy. Live fish and eyeballs? I'm not into that."

then he's spent a lot of time living out of a suitcase. To be perfectly honest, there are times when Shaun feels like he's missing out on things by not being a "normal" high school kid. But he believes the advantages far outweigh the disadvantages.

"It's all pretty good," Shaun says of his life as a pro snowboarder. "I mean, my friends in school are reading about ancient civilizations and buildings and temples, and that sort of thing, and I'm getting to walk around in them. That's kind of cool."

Short and slight, with red hair and freckles and an impish grin, Shaun is deceptively boyish. But ask any of his fellow competitors on the pro snowboarding circuit, and they'll tell you that appearances mean almost nothing. Shaun has the poise and talent of a veteran athlete and the imagination of a true artist. That combination has proved to be almost unbeatable. Producers of snowboarding videos and video games clamor for his services not only because he's so good at inventing tricks, but because he soars to incredible heights. Like a gymnast, Shaun's diminutive stature makes his acrobatic moves even more impressive.

But he's not just a showman. Shaun is also a serious competitor who continues to shred the opposition. In the winter of 2002, for example, he won a gold medal in slopestyle at the world snowboarding championships and a pair of silver medals at the Winter X Games. Not bad for a fifteen-year-old. But for Shaun, it's only the beginning. There's so much more he wants to accomplish.

"I want to win an Olympic event," he says. "That would be amazing. I want to win a big-air event, and I'd like to do a 180° flip in the pipe. There's still so much more I have to learn."

It's hard to imagine Shaun getting better and smarter, but it's bound to happen. And when it does…well, as Terje Haakonsen would say, "Scary."

And that's just on snow. A lot of skateboarders, and skateboarding fans, are just waiting for the day when Shaun devotes more time to his second sport. Among his most vocal supporters is Tony Hawk, who thinks Shaun could still be one of the best in the world.

"Shaun is the dark horse of vert skateboarding," says Hawk. "Most of the top skaters widely regard him as a prodigy, but you rarely see him at the big events."

That could soon change. Shaun still skates an average of three hours each day and has already promised to make an appearance at the 2003 Summer X Games. Don't be surprised if he winds up with a gold medal dangling from his neck.

"I thought about trying to go this year (in 2002), but some snowboarding things came up so I wasn't able to make it to the qualifiers," Shaun explains. "But next year I definitely plan to be there."

In the meantime, Shaun is doing his best to adjust to life in the spotlight. Snowboarding and skateboarding have taken Shaun all over the world. He's made friends and fans in such faraway places as Norway, France, and Austria.

But perhaps his favorite country to visit is Japan, where snowboarding has become extremely popular in recent years and athletes such as Shaun are mobbed by fans seeking autographs and handshakes. At first, the attention was a bit overwhelming for Shaun, but as he's gotten older, he's learned how to deal with it.

"Sometimes it's hard growing up in the spotlight because I always have to perform, even when I don't feel that good," Shaun wrote on his internet web site. "But it's helped me learn to keep pushing myself. It's also cool when kids recognize me — but it's weird, too, because they know all about you and you don't know anything about them. I appreciate my fans, though, and I always try to be cool to them. I try to be nice to everyone I meet."